I0617432

ISBN: 979-8-9893025-1-2
Publisher: Edward Chisolm
Cover and Interior Design: Shiela Alejandro

I dedicate this book to all of the amazing, little black boys who are sometimes "invisible" to this world. On this day, I support you, I admire you, and I affirm you. As quiet as it is kept, the world needs all you have to offer. And so does the Creator. I want each of you to embrace the unique, special, gifted, resilient, and powerful person God has made you.

Black Love, Black Peace & Black Power!
Edward Chisolm

By Edward Chisolm

This book is about inspiration. This book is about encouragement.
This book is about affirmation.
26 Words
26 Affirmations

They Call Me Mr...

Anointed	Nice
Blessed	Obedient
Considerate	Pure
Dependable	Quality
Excellent	Righteous
Fearless	Sensitive
Gifted	Truthful
Humble	Unique
Intelligent	Victory
Joy	Wisdom
Kindness	X Ray
Love	Young
Motivated	Zeal

"I am invisible because they refuse to see me"
- Ralph Ellison

Affirmation 1

They call me **Mr. Anointed...**
A once in a life time gift from God
for the whole world to see,
I am smart and funny, as special as I can be.

1 John 2:20

Affirmation 2

They call me **Mr. Blessed...**
Forgiven, fortunate, and highly favored as one can be,
I am so happy that God looked down with love at
little ole me.

Psalm 146:5

Affirmation 3

They call me **Mr. Considerate...**
For I care about you, and I care about me, I am God sent
so, I care about everybody.

1 Corinthians 12:25

Affirmation 4

They call me **Mr. Dependable...**
I am as faithful as I can be
when it comes to the important stuff of life
you can always count on me.

Luke 12:42

Affirmation 5

They call me **Mr. Excellent...**
Everything I do has
excellence as its name
reason being is because
excellence is my game.

Daniel 1:20

Affirmation 6

They call me **Mr. Fearless...**
I am confident in myself; I fear nothing or no one.
Whatever I put my mind to do
I always get the job done.

2 Timothy 1:7

Affirmation 7

They call me **Mr. Gifted...**
I am gifted by the Creator, there is absolutely nothing
I cannot do. I share my time, my treasures, and my
talents, especially for saints like you!

1 Peter 4:10

Affirmation 8

They call me **Mr. Humble...**
I practice humility daily because the meek will surely inherit the earth.
I am as humble as I can be. I've been this way ever since birth.

Ephesians 4:2

Affirmation 9

They call me **Mr. Intelligent...**
I am as smart as a whip,
reading lots of interesting books
makes me hip.

Luke 2:52

Affirmation 10

They call me **Mr. Joy...**
I am a joyful soul, happy as I can be, sharing happiness
with the world as far as the eyes can see.

James 1:2

Affirmation 11

They call me **Mr. Kindness...**
I am kind, gentle, and soft hearted always willing to lend a
helping hand. This is a trait I will keep for sure once I become a man.

Ephesians 4:32

Affirmation 12

They call me **Mr. Love...**
I got much love for the world
and much love for my fellow man.
I am determined to spread agape love all over this land.

1 Corinthians 16:14

Affirmation 13

They call me **Mr. Motivated...**
I am super motivated, that's one thing
about me you need to know.
I am skilled, willing, and equipped.
So Ready, Set, Go!

Colossians 3:23

Affirmation 14

They call me **Mr. Nice...**
That's the word that describes me
acting like Jesus is who I want to be.

Galatians 6:10

Affirmation 15

They call me **Mr. Obedient...**
I do whatever I can to please my parents and my God,
Like doing my chores, my homework, and even raking the yard.

Colossians 3:20

Affirmation 16

They call me **Mr. Pure...**
One day I will see God
Cus I've got love in my heart
My family I adore
We shall never part.

Matthew 5:8

Affirmation 17

They call me **Mr. Quality...**
Sir Quality is what they call me, helping people every
chance I get, like a good Samaritan
there is never a stranger I have met.

Exodus 31:3

Affirmation 18

They call me **Mr. Righteous...**
Because I do what is right
I do it because it is right,
and then I do it right.

Psalm 112:6

Affirmation 19

They call me **Mr. Sensitive...**
Meek as a lamb, tender as a dove
I share my love from heaven above.

John 11:35

Affirmation 20

They call me **Mr. Truthful...**
I am truthful because respect is important to me
an honest person is who I always want to be.

John 8:32

Affirmation 21

They call me **Mr. Unique...**
Nobody else is quite like me
I have my own style, swagger, and grace,
I live my life at my own pace.

Psalm 139:14

Affirmation 22

They call me **Mr. Victory...**
I am known as Mr. Victory because
I love to win. I give my very best to everything I am in.

Philippians 4:13

Affirmation 23

I am known as **Mr. Wisdom...**
They call me Mr. Wisdom cus
Intelligence is my name
Smart as a whip...yeah, I got game!

Proverbs 2:6

Affirmation 24

They call me **Mr. X-Ray...**
Because I see things other people don't
With discernment and a third eye,
I am willing to do what other people won't.

Matthew 6:22

Affirmation 25

They call me **Mr. Young...**
Because I am young, gifted, and black,
There is nothing I can't do,
There is nothing that I lack.

1 Timothy 4:12

Affirmation 26

They call me **Mr. Zeal...**
I am excited today and compassionate about what I am called to do,
to help my family, my community, and all of my friends, too.

Romans 12:11

Affirmation Scriptures

Affirmation 1 Anointed
"But you have an anointing from the Holy One, and you know all things"
1 John 2:20

Affirmation 2 Blessed
"Blessed is he who has the God of Jacob for his help" Psalm 146:5

Affirmation 3 Considerate
"So that there should be no division in the body, but that the parts should have the same care for one another" 1 Corinthians 12:25

Affirmation 4 Dependable
"Who then is the faithful and wise steward" Luke 12:42

Affirmation 5 Excellent
"In all matter of wisdom and understanding, he found them ten times better" Daniel 1:20

Affirmation 6 Fearless
"For God has not given us a spirit of fear, but of power and love, and self-control" 2 Timothy 1:7

Affirmation 7 Gifted
"As everyone has received a gift, even so serve one another with it"
1 Peter 4:10

Affirmation 8 Humble
"With all humility, meekness, and patience, bearing with one another in love" Ephesians 4:2

Affirmation 9 Intelligent
"And Jesus increased in wisdom and in stature, and in favor with God and man." Luke 2:52

Affirmation 10 Joy
"My brothers, count it all joy when you fall into diverse temptations" James 1:2

Affirmation 11 Kindness
"And be kind to one another, tenderhearted, forgiving one another." Ephesians 4:32

Affirmation 12   Love
"Let all that you do be done with love" 1 Corinthians 16:14

Affirmation 13 Motivated
"And whatever you do, do it heartily, as for the Lord and not for men" Colossians 3:23

Affirmation 14 Nice
"Therefore, as we have opportunity, let us do good to all people" Galatians 6:10

Affirmation 15 Obedient
"Children obey your parents in all things, for this is well pleasing to the Lord" Colossians 3:20

Affirmation 16 Pure
"Blessed are the pure in heart, for they shall see God" Matthew 5:8

Affirmation 17 Quality
"I have filled him with the Spirit of God in wisdom, in understanding in knowledge, and in all manner of craftmanship" Exodus 31:3

Affirmation 18 Righteous
"Surely the righteous man shall not be moved" Psalm 112:6

Affirmation 19 Sensitive
"Jesus wept" John 11:35

Affirmation 20 Truthful
"You shall know the truth, and the truth shall set you free" John 8:32

Affirmation 21 Unique
"I will praise you , for You made me with fear and wonder, marvelous are Your works" Psalm 139:14

Affirmation 22 Victory
"I can do all things because of Christ who strengthens me" Philippians 4:13

Affirmation 23 Wisdom
"For the Lord gives wisdom; out of His mouth comes knowledge and understanding" Proverbs 2:6

Affirmation 24 X-Ray
"The light of the body is the eye, if your eye is clear, your whole body will be full of light" Matthew 6:22

Affirmation 25 Young

"Let no one despise your youth, but be an example to the believers in speech, in conduct, in love, in spirit, in faith, and in purity"
1 Timothy 4:12

Affirmation 26 Zeal

"Do not be lazy in diligence, be fervent in spirit, serve the Lord"
Romans 12:11

ABOUT THE AUTHOR

Edward was born into a family of four in 1959 in Hardeeville, South Carolina. Edward can be best described as a warm, caring, generous, kind, and considerate man of God. He is a humble man who loves the Lord. Edward is the extremely proud father of two beautiful adult children, Corey (37) and Michelle (35).

Edward is a dedicated and powerful teacher of God's Word and a certified instructor in Christian Education. Edward is the author of several other books, including 40 Daily Thoughts for the Christian Soldier (Volumes 1 & 2), 23 Daily Thoughts for the Young Christian Soldier, From the Diary of a Black Man's Mind: From Demagogue to Disciple, and Manna All Day. In his spare time, Edward enjoys watching sports, and movies, listening to music, traveling, and of course, studying and teaching God's Word. His motto is: "Do Your Best, and God will do the Rest!"

www.ingramcontent.com/pod-product-compliance
Lightning Source LLC
Chambersburg PA
CBHW041558120626
46551CB00002B/248